W9-BVQ-004

Asia

GARY DREVITCH

Children's Press®
An Imprint of Scholastic Inc.
New York   Toronto   London   Auckland   Sydney
Mexico City   New Delhi   Hong Kong
Danbury, Connecticut

Content Consultant

Michael Robinson
Professor, Department of East Asian Languages and Cultures
Indiana University
Bloomington, Indiana

Library of Congress Cataloging-in-Publication Data

Drevitch, Gary, 1968-
  Asia / by Gary Drevitch.
      p. cm. -- (A true book)
  Includes index.
ISBN-13: 978-0-531-16865-3 (lib. bdg.)
           978-0-531-21827-3 (pbk.)
ISBN-10: 0-531-16865-4 (lib. bdg.)
           0-531-21827-9 (pbk.)

  1. Asia--Juvenile literature. I. Title. II. Series.

  DS5.D74 2008
  950--dc22

  2008000266

Produced by Weldon Owen Education Inc.

2 3 4 5 6 7 8 9 10 R 18 17 16 15 14 13 12 11

Find the Truth!

Everything you are about to read is true *except* for one of the sentences on this page.

Which one is **TRUE**?

T or F   Buddhism began in Japan.

T or F   The giant panda eats only bamboo.

Find the answers in this book.

Contents

THE **BIG** TRUTH!

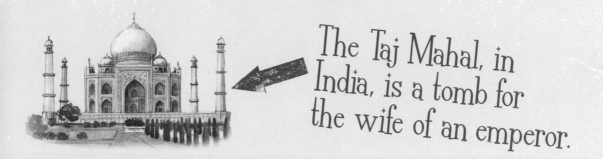

The Taj Mahal, in India, is a tomb for the wife of an emperor.

The White Water River, China, is fed by melted snow from Jade Dragon Snow Mountain. People cross the river on foot, horses, or yaks.

CHAPTER 1

Biggest and Busiest

Asia is the biggest continent on Earth. It also has the most people. In the north, frozen plains and evergreen forests stretch for thousands of miles. In the southeast, there are tropical rain forests. In central Asia are rugged mountains. Asia has some of the most crowded cities in the world. Yet there are places where no person has ever set foot.

The Asian yak is related to the American bison.

Snow-Capped Mountains

Asia has more mountains than any other continent. The Caucasus Mountains lie between the Black and Caspian seas. They form part of the border between Asia and Europe.

The Kunlun mountain range is one of the longest in Asia. It stretches more than 1,850 miles (3,000 kilometers) across central China.

On the border of China and Nepal are the Himalayas (hih-muh-LAY-uhz). Their name means "house of snow" in Sanskrit, the ancient language of India. The Himalayas have hundreds of snowy peaks. Many of them are more than 22,000 feet (6,700 meters) high. Mount Everest, the world's tallest mountain, rises 29,035 feet (8,850 meters) above sea level. That is nearly six miles (9.7 kilometers) high!

Asia

N
W · E
S

Arctic Ocean

Arctic Circle

Siberia

Russia
(Europe)

Russia
(Asia)

EUROPE

Caspian Sea

Kazakhstan

Mongolia

Gobi Desert

Caucasus

Black Sea

1
2 3
12
13

Turkey

Turkmenistan

14

Kunlun Mountains

China

Japan

Pacific Ocean

*editerranean
Sea*

Syria

4 5

6 7

Iraq

Afghanistan

Iran

Himalayas

Bhutan

South
Korea

North
Korea

8

Saudi
Arabia

9

10

11

Pakistan

Nepal

17

Myanmar

23

Arabian Desert

Oman

India

19

Thailand

18

Egypt

Yemen

20

Philippines

AFRICA

16

15 ☐

22 ☐

Equator

☐ 21

Malaysia

Indonesia

Indian Ocean

East Timor

Key to Numbered Countries

1 Georgia	9 Bahrain	16 Sri Lanka
2 Armenia	10 Qatar	17 Bangladesh
3 Azerbaijan	11 United Arab	18 Vietnam
4 Cyprus	Emirates	19 Laos
5 Lebanon	12 Uzbekistan	20 Cambodia
6 Israel	13 Kyrgyzstan	21 Singapore
7 Jordan	14 Tajikistan	22 Brunei
8 Kuwait	15 Maldives	23 Taiwan

Forests of the South

In Southeast Asia, rain forests cover large parts of the land. Thick layers of trees, vines, and plants grow in the warm, wet climate. The rain forests have some of the most diverse plant and animal life in the world. **Orangutans**, tigers, and parrots all live in Asia's rain forests. There are also hundreds of species of reptiles and insects.

Rafflesia (ra-FLEE-zhuh) flowers, from Southeast Asia, can be more than three feet (90 centimeters) wide.

A smell like rotting meat attracts insects to some rafflesias!

Unfortunately, large parts of the rain forests have been cleared for farming and mining. Trees are also cut down for lumber. **Deforestation** has permanently wiped out thousands of species of plants and animals. Today, some governments in the region are working to protect the forests that remain.

In the Philippines, some forest loss has led to landslides.

11

Tundra

Far from the warm, wet rain forests are the freezing, windswept regions of northern Russia. *Tundra* is the Russian word for "treeless plain." Most of the tundra lies inside the **Arctic Circle**. Few people live there, but there are many animals. These include wild reindeer, arctic foxes, and hares.

Wild reindeer roam the Russian tundra.

The Trans-Siberian Railroad is the world's longest railroad. It takes almost a week to travel its entire length.

Forests of the North

South of the tundra is the taiga (TYE-guh). This is a vast **evergreen** forest. It stretches across northern Russia to the Pacific Coast.

Northern Russia, or Siberia, is rich in resources. Coal, lumber, oil, diamonds, gold, and platinum are all found there. The Trans-Siberian Railroad crosses the region. It is 5,600 miles (9,012 kilometers) long.

In some parts of Asia, people build houses on stilts as a practical solution to living on frequently flooded terrain.

CHAPTER 2

Living in Asia

The way people live depends largely on where they live. In Asia, people cope with a wide range of climates and conditions. In desert areas, people struggle with intense heat and prolonged **droughts**. In **fertile** river valleys, people are able to farm. In rugged mountain terrain, getting around is difficult. In coastal cities, many people work in factories that produce goods for export.

This fishing village on stilts is built on a tidal plain in Thailand.

Sand and Snow

Asia has several deserts. The Arabian Peninsula contains the Arabian Desert, the world's second largest. Few people live in this hot desert. However, the peninsula's east and west coasts support farming.

The Gobi is a cold winter desert. It lies in China and Mongolia. Snow blankets it in winter. Summer temperatures can reach 113 °F (45 °C). The people of the Gobi are nomadic herders.

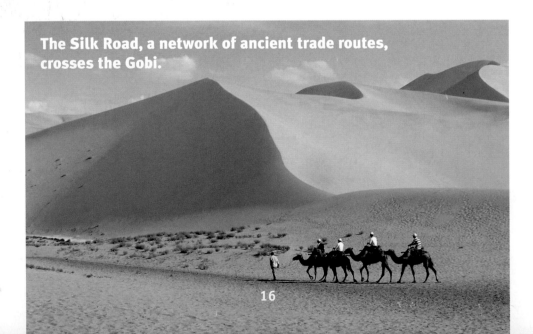

The Silk Road, a network of ancient trade routes, crosses the Gobi.

Desert People

Bedouins (BEHD-u-wihnz) have survived in the
Arabian Desert for centuries. In the past, they
moved from place to place working as traders
or herders. They lived in tents made of goat hair,
called *bayts* (BITES). Bedouins relied on camels
for transportation, meat, and milk.
They used camel droppings for fuel.
Some Bedouins today still live
in the traditional way.

During the summer monsoon season, heavy rains and floods are a part of daily life in India.

Stormy Seasons

Monsoons and cyclones are two kinds of wild weather that are common in southern Asia. Monsoons are strong seasonal winds. In winter, they bring cool weather from the east. In summer, monsoons blow from the west. They bring warm air and heavy rains that often cause flooding. Cyclones are hurricanes. Huge cyclones, called typhoons, often damage property and even cause deaths.

Tsunamis (tsoo-NAH-mees) pose a threat to people in coastal areas. A tsunami is a large, strong wave system. It is usually caused by an earthquake on the ocean floor. Although tsunamis occur only rarely, most of the biggest in history have occurred in Asia. In 2004, a massive tsunami smashed into Indonesia, Sri Lanka, India, the Maldives, and Thailand. It caused more than 280,000 deaths.

Blue-and-white tsunami warning signs are used all over the world.

Since the 2004 tsunami disaster, many countries do regular tsunami safety drills.

River Market

Some of Thailand's major cities are built along winding rivers where canals serve as streets. In these places, there is a long tradition of floating markets. One of the country's most famous markets is in a small town called Damnoen Saduak, near Bangkok. Tourists from around the world come to the market. They hop from boat to boat to buy goods.

Waterways

Farmers and other vendors steer long, narrow boats through a series of canals to get to the market. Here they trade produce or sell to shoppers in boats and on the shore.

Fruit and Flowers

Most boats sell local produce, such as fruit, vegetables, and flowers. Others sell freshly made hot noodle dishes. Some sell items such as tools, twine, or textiles.

Monkeys can be seen all over the city of New Delhi, India.

CHAPTER 3

Wildest Wildlife

The pangolin, or scaly anteater, hunts for insects at night.

Asia is home to a huge variety of animal species. They include some of the rarest species in the world. However, not all of Asia's wildlife lives in the wild. In towns and cities all over Asia, wild animals coexist with people. Some animals are used for work. Others have simply gotten used to living among humans. As in other parts of the world today, many animal species in Asia are **endangered**.

Great Cats

Long ago, both lions and tigers roamed Asia. The Asian lion once ranged as far as the Mediterranean Sea! Today, Asia has only a small lion population left. It lives in a protected reserve in India.

Tigers are a highly adaptable species. They live in snowy Siberia. They also live in hotter areas, such as Bangladesh and India. Although tigers are endangered, programs are in place to boost the wild population.

Tigers are the largest cats in the world.

The population of snow leopards is increasing in some conservation areas.

Unlike most other big cats, snow leopards cannot roar.

The snow leopard is at home in the mountains of central and southern Asia. Hunting and deforestation have reduced its numbers drastically. The snow leopard has been protected since 1975. However, people still hunt it illegally. Many Asian countries have now set up reserves and protected habitats for their big cats.

Smart Giants

Because the Asian elephant is so intelligent and so big and strong, it has been widely **domesticated**. Ancient Indian armies rode into battle on trained elephants. For centuries, people have used them to carry heavy loads, for transportation, and in ceremonies. Today, the elephant's natural habitat has been reduced by deforestation. Large reserves have been set up to protect this endangered giant.

Some elephants are still used in the logging industry in Asia.

Rare Giants

In the wild, the giant panda lives only in China. It eats only bamboo. However, China has cut down many of its bamboo forests. This has placed the panda at risk. To help restore panda populations, China has now set up bamboo forest reserves. Corridors between the reserves allow pandas to move from one reserve to another in search of food.

Pandas often raise only one cub every several years. Breeding programs are attempting to improve panda reproduction.

The ancient civilization of the Indus River valley covered an enormous area.

CHAPTER 4

Where It All Began

Thousands of years ago, three of the world's earliest **civilizations** emerged in Asia. In each case, people established settlements in fertile river valleys. They grew crops and domesticated animals. They invented forms of writing and organized social groups. They crafted goods and traded among themselves. Settlements grew into the first towns and cities.

The Indus River civilization even had water and sewer systems.

Three River Valleys

About 7,000 years ago, the civilization of Mesopotamia (mehs-uh-puh-TAY-mee-uh) developed. It grew up between the Tigris and Euphrates (yoo-FRAY-teez) rivers. Today, this region is part of Iraq. Mesopotamians developed methods of **irrigation**, so their crops could survive dry periods. As farming became more efficient, some people could pursue other occupations and crafts such as pottery. Mesopotamians were the first people to use the wheel.

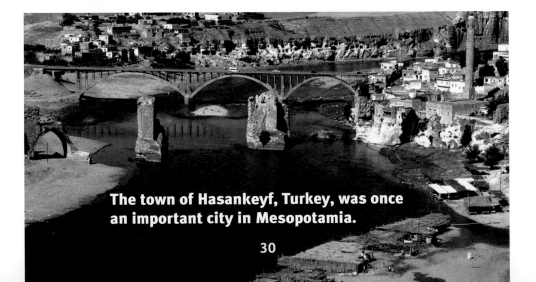

The town of Hasankeyf, Turkey, was once an important city in Mesopotamia.

The Yellow River in China is named for the yellow soil it carries.

The Indus River is in present-day Pakistan and northwest India. About 4,500 years ago, the Indus Valley was the home of the Harappan civilization. The Harappans were the first to use dikes. Dikes are high walls to prevent flooding. The Harappans also developed a system of weights and measures.

About 3,700 years ago, people in China's Yellow River valley wove silk cloth and made pottery. They devised a complex system of writing. Modern Chinese writing is based on that system.

Birthplace of Religions

Several major world religions developed in Asia. One of the oldest is Hinduism, the main religion in India. There are many Hindu gods. Hindus believe that a person's soul is reborn in a new body after death.

The Buddhist religion began in northern India. Its teachings stress the need to discipline your mind to face challenges in life.

The three main **monotheistic** religions developed in the Middle East. In fact, Christianity, Judaism, and Islam share a source in the same ancient sacred texts.

Time Line of Faith

1800 B.C.

Judaism begins in today's Israel. It is one of the first religions to worship only one god.

500 B.C.

Buddhism begins. It is based on the teachings of Siddhartha Gautama. He is later called the Buddha.

The teachings of Confucius still have great influence on ideas and life in China, Korea, Japan, and Vietnam. Confucius lived about 2,500 years ago in China. You probably know his "golden rule." It says to treat others as you would like to be treated.

Shinto has existed for about 2,500 years in Japan. It is based on a belief in sacred spirits connected with nature. Shinto is often practiced alongside other beliefs, such as Confucianism and Buddhism.

About 30 A.D.

Christianity begins in Israel. The followers of Jesus Christ spread his ideas throughout the Roman Empire.

622 A.D.

Islam is founded in what is now Saudi Arabia. The prophet Muhammad teaches about a single god, named Allah.

Long ago, the Great Wall of China was built to protect China's northern border from invaders. Today, visitors from all over the world flock to see it.

CHAPTER 5

Ancient Empires

Asia was home to several powerful ancient empires. For centuries, high mountains or vast deserts separated groups of people. Groups or clans lived under constant threat of attack. Eventually, strong leaders united rival groups. They built powerful kingdoms. In China, Qin Shi Huangdi (chin shirr hwong-dee) unified China's warring states in 221 B.C. He declared himself China's first emperor.

Emperor Qin Shi Huangdi began the first part of the Great Wall in 220 B.C.

Crossroads of the World

The area around Turkey and the Middle East has long been a site of conflicts. One reason is that it includes access to important trade routes over both land and water.

Alexander the Great of Greece led his armies far into Asia. By 323 B.C., his empire extended to India. Later, the Romans conquered much of this area.

Alexander the Great conquered the Persian empire in 330 B.C. Persepolis, in present-day Iran, was its capital.

Karakorum was the capital of the Mongol Empire. This Buddhist monastery was established there in the 1200s.

The religion of Islam spread rapidly after its founding. As it spread, so did an Islamic Empire. By about 750 A.D., this empire reached from India to Spain. Along with their faith, Muslims spread advanced knowledge of math, science, and medicine.

In the early 1200s, the Mongol tribes of northeast Asia were united by the leader Genghis Khan (JEHNG-gihs KAHN). The Mongol Empire grew to be the largest land empire in the history of the world. It covered most of present-day Asia and lasted for nearly 100 years.

Japan is one of the most crowded
countries in the world. Tokyo's
commuter trains carry more than
ten million people every day.

CHAPTER 6

Today's Asia

Asia has changed hugely in just the past few decades. Some Asian countries have modernized rapidly. Several have become leading exporters. They produce goods such as cars, computers, clothing, and cameras. China and India now have booming **economies**. They are challenging the position of the United States as the largest economy in the world.

⬅ During rush hour in Tokyo, "oshiya," or pushers, help squeeze people into train cars.

Culture Crazes

In Asia, pop culture is big business. Millions of Japanese manga comic books, graphic novels, and animated movies have been exported to the United States. Movies from Hong Kong have fans in many countries. South Asians living all over the world flock to see Bollywood movies from India.

Manga-style comic books have been translated into English since the 1980s.

Manga-style comic books are read from right to left, the same way Japanese is written.

Bollywood

The *B* in *Bollywood* stands for Bombay, India.
That is the old name for the city of Mumbai.
This is where most of India's movies are made.
Bollywood studios are the busiest in the world.
They produce 800 movies a year—that's twice
as many as Hollywood makes!
Bollywood stars sometimes
work on four movies
at once! India's most
popular movies
are musicals,
with romantic
plots and
colorful
costumes.

The oldest teahouse in Shanghai, China, contrasts with modern skyscrapers.

Asia Grows

Asia faces the same challenges as many other parts of the world. As Asian countries become more modern, they become more crowded. Growing populations often mean less space for native plants and animals. The challenge is to find the balance—between old and new, between cities and nature, between globalization and local needs. ★

True Statistics

Size: About 17,039,000 square miles (44,131,000 square kilometers)

Greatest distance east to west: 6,000 miles (9,700 kilometers)

Greatest distance north to south: 5,400 miles (8,690 kilometers)

Population: More than 4 billion

Number of Countries: 50

Life expectancy (selected countries): Japan, 82; Israel, 80; Saudi Arabia, 76; North Korea, 72; India, 69; Yemen, 63; Laos, 56

Followers of Major Religions: Muslims, 892 million; Hindus, 845 million; Buddhists, 370 million; Christians, 341 million

Did you find the truth?

F Buddhism began in Japan.

T The giant panda eats only bamboo.

Resources

Books

Allison, Carol J. *Mighty Earth.* (Shockwave: Science). Danbury, CT: Children's Press, 2008.

Aretha, David. *Discovering Asia's Land, People, and Wildlife* (Continents of the World). Berkeley Heights, NJ: MyReportLinks.com, 2004.

Dalmatian Press. *Pandas and Other Animals of Asia* (Nature). Atlanta: 2007.

Foster, Leila Merrell. *Asia* (Continents). Portsmouth, NH: Heinemann, 2006.

Fowler, Allan. *Asia* (Rookie Read-About Geography). New York: Children's Press, 2002.

Kalman, Bobbie and Sjonger, Rebecca. *Explore Asia* (Explore the Continents). New York: Crabtree Children's Books, 2007.

Morley, Jacqueline. *You Wouldn't Want to Work on the Great Wall of China!: Defenses You'd Rather Not Build.* Danbury, CT: Franklin Watts, 2006.

Morrison, Ian. *Skiing in the Desert: Asian Innovation* (Shockwave: Science). Danbury, CT: Children's Press, 2008.

Organizations and Web Sites

Ask Asia
http://www.askasia.org/kids/
Play games, read stories, try out Asian languages, and learn about Asian culture and art.

History for Kids
http://www.historyforkids.org/learn/westasia/
Learn all about the Mesopotamians, Sumerians, Egyptians, and more.

Asia's Tsunami
http://www.timeforkids.com/TFK/tsunami
Read all about the 2004 tsunami, read kids' letters about it, and find out how you can help victims today.

Places to Visit

The Metropolitan Museum of Art
1000 Fifth Ave
New York, NY 10028-0198
(212) 535 7710
metmuseum.org/Works_of_Art/asian_art
The museum has one of the world's largest collections of Asian art.

Asian Art Museum
200 Larkin St
San Francisco, CA 94102
(415) 581 3500
www.asianart.org
The museum's galleries hold collections of ancient and modern art from across Asia.

Important Words

Arctic Circle – an imaginary line on the globe that encloses the North Pole and the Arctic regions

civilization – a highly developed society, usually with a form of written language, division of occupations, and different social levels

deforestation – loss of forest due to clearing and cutting of trees

domesticate – to change an animal's natural way of life so that it can live closely with people and be of advantage to them

drought – a long period with little or no rainfall

economy – the system in which goods and services are produced, bought, and sold

endangered – close to being one of the last of its kind left on Earth

evergreen – a bush or tree that has green leaves year round

fertile (FUR-tuhl) – able to produce crops

irrigation (ear-uh-GAY-shun) – the supplying of water to farmland, usually by human-made methods

monotheistic – having to do with the belief in a single god

orangutan (uh-RANG-uh-tan) – a large ape with long, reddish-brown hair, native to Borneo and Sumatra

Index

Page numbers in **bold** indicate illustrations.

About the Author

Gary Drevitch has written many books, textbooks, and magazine articles for young people. He loves to read and write about far-off places and ancient empires. If he could go anywhere in Asia, he'd go to Jerusalem, in Israel, and to China, to visit the tomb of China's first emperor. Gary lives in New York City with his wife and three children.

PHOTOGRAPHS: Digital Vision (p. 11); Getty Images (p. 22; pp. 27–28; p. 30; p. 41); iStockphoto (© Adam Korzekwa, Pearl Tower, p. 5; © Gina Smith, p. 19; © Richard Robinson, Buddha, p. 32; © Steve Humphreys, p. 16; © Valerie Shanin, p. 36; © Vova Pomortzeff, p. 25); Photo New Zealand (age fotostock/ Walter Allgoewer, p. 14); Photodisc (p. 24); Photolibrary (cover; p. 6; p. 18; p. 34; p. 42); © Rosemanios flickr. com (p. 31); © Seth Coleman/flickr.com (p. 38); Stock.XCHNG (back cover; Judaic star, p. 32; mosque, p. 33); Tranz (Corbis, p. 10; p. 12; p. 17; p. 20; p. 26; p. 37; p. 40; Photoshot, p. 13)

The publisher would like to thank Rosemanios for the photograph on page 31 and Seth Coleman for the photograph on page 38.

OCT   2011